The Inner Realm

Namrata Singh

BookLeaf
Publishing

India | USA | UK

Presentation by *BookLeaf Publishing*

Web: www.bookleafpub.com

E-mail: info@bookleafpub.com

ISBN: 9789363318106

First edition 2024

In the loving memory of my mother, Jasbir Kaur, who infused in me the art of intuition and poetry writing.

Her blessings continue to flow in my life, much like the love of Mother Nature.

PREFACE

When I chanced upon BookLeaf Publishing's poetry writing challenge, I immediately decided to take it up. I didn't think twice because getting my book of poems published is a dream I have been harbouring since childhood.

Even in my early days of rhyming, nature inspired me in many ways. Naturally, given that I enjoyed the privilege of living amid sylvan surroundings in the pre-internet era, I was more inclined to write about nature.

I also took up this challenge to stoke my creative brain to help me channel my thoughts, which otherwise were going unwritten and unheard due to the paucity of time.

But writing continuously for 21 days is certainly challenging. There weren't too many ready or unused poems in my kitty. Whatever I write is usually posted on social media. So I began the journey with the low-hanging fruits. I plucked the first few thoughts that gave me the raw ideas. I put them into words and sentences and then chiselled them with my creativity, converting them into poems.

Once I got started, it was like a self-powered churning mill that began to dish out poems one after the other. Intriguing and interesting anecdotes that were always at the back of my mind got a chance to now be heard. The stories, which otherwise formed part of my journaling notes, were dusted and drafted into poems.

The busy world does not have the time to spare for its own, let alone the goings on in the lives of birds, trees, and the unseen, the unknown. I began to dive deeper into my subconscious mind to mine precious moments that were buried under the dust of time and were waiting to be found and unveiled.

When I saw the initial poems processed and packaged, it evoked a deep sense of duty and commitment to take this task to its logical conclusion. Yes, I had to do it, come what may! Many moments of joy and sorrow surfaced as I started writing more. These 21 days of digging deeper and going into nooks and corners of my heart and mind that I had forgotten existed were no less than a detox. My mind, spirit, and body now feel light and refreshed. Some doors and windows that were slammed shut were opened creakingly to let in some light, some freshness. What reeked of negativity got released through the magic of converting thoughts into words and words into meaningful poems.

My mind, my soul, and every cell of my body are now renewed. I feel rejuvenated! I realised there was an ocean inside my consciousness, which found an outlet thanks to the poetry writing challenge. I have poured my heart and soul into this.

The challenge has given me great motivation to continue writing poetry, a skill I believe is intrinsic to me. But I had lost it somewhere along the way. I am now happy to pick up the threads from where I left off.

I hope you all enjoy reading these poems. They're not just words; they're drops of my emotions. They're pieces of puzzles that the mysteries of life present us with. They are stories that will bring a smile to your face. They'll appeal to your aesthetic senses. They'll make you think and, in turn, trigger your creative right brain.

Happy reading!

Namrata Singh

TABLE OF CONTENTS

CHAPTER 1 :

INSPIRATION FROM STARS

Starlight

A surreal glow in the sky
A glimmer of happiness on my face
The light within
Escapes the eyes
When the first star rises
to connect with the iris
in a sublime caress.

Stars that shine

The inevitable rain
left drops of little stars
on my window pane.
Little precious stars,
to my eye's delight,
shone in bright sunlight.
Stars in broad daylight!
With the advent of the night,
and in the diminishing light
little stars vanished.
Vanishing along with them
were the twinkling stars
in my eyes,
until I looked up to see
a star-studded sky!

Walking on stars

Rising high
in the sky
above the ordinary
walking on stars,
I look down with telescope eyes
to find the oceans glittering
in the light of the sun,
shimmering
like the stars in the sky.

A beacon

On a strange, long road
I am not alone
A star up there
Is quietly walking
along with me,
Sweeping aside
darkness
projecting its light
Enlightening my vision
Etching out a path
Bringing it into sight
Enlivening the moments
Leading the way
Starry and bright

Unbounded

Earlier, when I saw
the stars in the sky
It kindled an ambition
To reach out
And touch the sky.
When I visually amassed them,
plucking them with my eyes,
I could feel the warmth,
the light emanating from my eyes.
Now, when I walk on stars
I can see an unlimited sky!

Starry-eyed

It's not that the stars in the sky lack any lustre,
The ones my eyes behold,
are precious!
I see stars in broad daylight!
I tend to them with love and care
I affirm their existence.
I visualise conversations,
holding them dearly and further nurturing their
richness.
It's not that the stars in the sky are less alluring,
the ones my eyes grasp tenderly,
are priceless!
Entwined with my ambitions,
sky-high,
my dreams of achieving greatness

that my hopes don't belie,
I engage the stars in my eyes,
moulding them into what I perceive through my
inner eye.
It's not that the stars in the sky are less
mysterious,
The ones my eyes hold graciously,
are inexplicably magical!

Star, you there?

When I see you twinkle,
Are you really there, little one?
Or is it just an image of your past
which has travelled a million years
to flash onto Earth's horizon?
My, you sparkle even after you're long gone!
When I see a blank space in the sky,
Could there be a new star being born
in the womb of the cosmos?
Even as we fret over what's mine, what's yours.

CHAPTER 2 :

THE MYSTICAL & ESOTERIC

Epiphany

When you clearly see what was so far hidden,
Uncovering the veil from the enigmatic black
hole riddle,
Realisation dawns in soft shades of pastel
It's just the surface
of an eternal cradle;
There's more to be seen.
There's more to be seen.

As above, so below

A sudden storm
brought the rain down,
creating puddles along the way.
These nano lakes stood their ground
alongside stony paver blocks, manicured lawns,
haughty towers and tall trees.
As I walked down these paths,
The sky walked along with me!
Patches of the sky appeared on the ground,
birds momentarily reflected their flight in these
water screens,
cottony clouds proudly peeked
at what they just created,
while tree branches drooped close enough
to check out their shiny leaves.

At that moment, the two worlds coexisted for me,
As above, so below.

Window to the unconscious mind

If you ever want to find me,
You will find me
sitting in my living room,
And though I'll be absorbed in my thoughts,
You'll find me
facing the window
that overlooks and is entirely covered by the
branches of a large neem
tree.

It's not just a window with a beautiful view of
the garden,
It's a window to my mind,
where thoughts get converted into words;
It's a doorway through which my inner eye
connects with the worlds.

When a bird flies by,
a thought crosses my mind.
When a crow comes knocking,
a message well travelled,
sits quietly,
waiting to be unravelled.

It's not just a window to admire the deep blue
sky,
and the robins hopping by;
It's a window that opens my soul to eternity.
When I feel lost,
Or I run out of ideas,
I just have to raise
my gaze
to the window.
Looking out of the window
gets me rewired
and inspired.

When I am stuck
by the writer's block,
I look out for prompts,
which surely get delivered,
just like the sprightly squirrel
who jumps over to check in;
Or the bunch of tattling sparrows
biding their time on the window pane
to escape the heavy rain.

When the wind drifts by,
shaking the branches of the tree,
a unique set of thoughts wafts into my being.
I also get enough food for thought,
when I see a crow feeding its fledgling;
Or when sunlight filters through the leaves,
creating patterns on the wall,
on display,
nature's shadow dancing.

When stillness pervades,
not a leaf shakes,
the cacophonous thoughts now settle,
allowing the empty mind to brood on the void,
naturally shifting the gaze inward.

And when the silence is broken by a bunch of
squabbling mynas,
It fuels my thinking tank to sprint ahead with
ideas.

A pleasant rain,
ushers in the earthy fragrance,
jogging my memory
to play sweet monsoon jingles.

A nostalgia-soaked mind
reminds

me to air some rhymes
lying as digital notes,
Rounding them off,
I enliven them
to be used,
Maybe in another season,
for another reason.

Reciprocity

I stare at a blank wall,
A mirror image of my mind.
Devoid of thoughts, colours,
Intertwined
In a harmonious relationship.
The two share
a familiarity bias.
The wall says nothing,
And the mind is quiet.
An understanding exists
Somewhere in sight.
As the mind
Begins to project
on the wall,
Streaming poetry
adorning it with gems
Embedding artistry

Into a delightful tapestry.
In reciprocity
Beauty and essence
gush in to fill my mind space.
Buoyant creativity
shines through my eyes,
reflecting the brightness
of the now beautifully embellished wall.
Hearty mutuality, arise.

Enigma

I am a blank page
For many
who try to gauge me.
Read me
if you can,
I am a story
laden in mystery.
Read me
in-between moments
surrounding fervent frenzy
when my eyes give away
In a conscientious way.
My eyes can reveal a hundred emotions
And hide as many.
Unravel what you can,
light a hundred incense sage,
if you will,
I remain for many
a blank page.
A confidante to many of different age
a secret keeper,
old style, vintage
layer on layer
form my foliage.
The world can, on its axis, spin;
To reach my core, my essence
First, fathom the storm within.

Singularity

Water droplets
translucent and pure
reflect light
in multiple hues
of red, yellow, blues
appearing
momentarily
disparate,
even though
water droplets
are identical,
all through,
much like souls
reflecting the same light.
Pure light
penetrates
each soul,
gets coloured
through
layers of varied perceptions
and discrimination
to appear diverse.
A prism of reality
or an illusion?
Purity
gets differentiated

Into apparent
distinct individuality.

Dreamer

You see a cloud,
I see a ray.
You fear the abyss,
I see a pathway.
A tree in a seed,
Water in clay.
Call it optimism,
Term it madness,
It's a spark of joy;
I perceive light
Even in the depths of darkness.

...and I let it be

When it finally appeared before me,
I stared at the moment unblinkingly;
A glimpse of eternity!
Or was I imagining?
No, I did not entertain that thought and let it be.
Staying firm in that infinite moment,
I held it in my gaze
Perpetually.
It was so close
I could touch the heart of the moment
I could see my reflection in it
I could see the whole universe in it!
Nothing mattered
Not work, no food, no train catching or cabbing.
It was just that moment and me in it.
As if I had merged with it,
The perceiver became the perceived.
I wanted to hold it,
forever.

Forever?
A desire to hold it?
The awareness of time
And the consciousness of being
Finally got me,
Detaching me from the perception that was
eternity.
The perceiver perceived the passing of
perpetuity…
… and I let it be.

Tarot

You moved your faltering fingers
over the fanned-out cards,
unconsciously pulling
one card after the other,
building on the layout.
Every card stitches together
a crucial past moment
with the present and the likely future.
Just like that,
stranger,
your life's story began to linger
before my inner eyes.
A snapshot of what emerged,
gradually,
in a piecemeal manner,
unveiled, deeply rooted moments
buried under the dust of time,
layer after layer__
the starting points,

the harbingers.
I could read your mind
even more clear;
some your eyes couldn't hide.
The solution you couldn't fathom,
is now near.
How could you not see it earlier?
At last, you got it,
There's no reason to fear!

The Fool

A mind, free, without a care
A burden light
So I can dare.
Not a worry
To which a thought
I can spare
I can leap anywhere,
Everywhere.
I have nothing to lose,
Nothing to share
The sun is with me
At the start of my journey.
Here, there, everywhere
Lies my potential
I sow the seeds of my future
At every step, with care.
My energy is unbounded
My heart doesn't skip a beat
To think which door will open
Which one will slam
The time is now for me
Now is where I am.

(Note: The Fool is a card in Tarot)

Free will

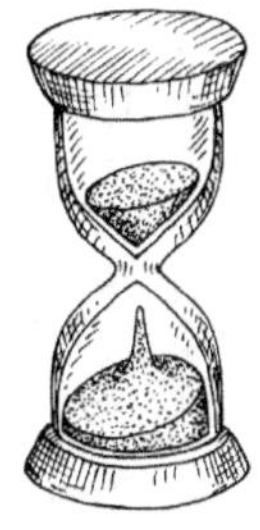

The lengthening shadow of the past
gave it an illusion of being bigger
than the present moment
and an indiscernible future.
The evanescent, fleeting present moment
didn't have enough time to last,
so it passed
on the baton to its future brethren
and succumbed to becoming the past.
The cavalier future,
Ever distant
mocked at the past and the present
with its audacity to remain evergreen,
a goalpost to which
all moments rush to switch,
but none reach.
The now recalcitrant past
haughtily told the future
"Don't past tense me, bro,
I am the lesson

you need to learn
to grow."
Caught between the two,
the present moment finally
grabbed the spotlight
to retain its glory.
Neither the past nor the future
is ceaseless,
it conjectured.
It's the free will in the present moment
that can truly liberate
one from the shadow of the past
and a promise of a future.

The fork

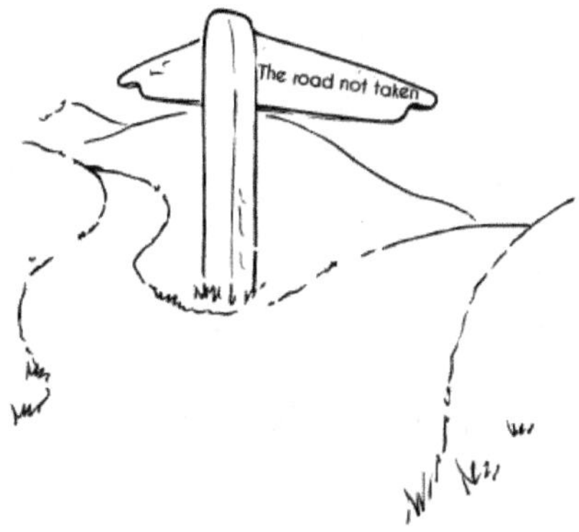

I cross to the side untrodden.
Though green, energizing, unrefined,
it contrasts with the depth of the flowering
valley I left behind.
My feet are rooted
but my mind drifts like clouds.
My dreams, grand
My ambitions, pinned to the stars,
bloom in far-off lands.
It haunts me,
as I walk about,
alone, upright,
In search of
the infinite.

CHAPTER 3 :

MOMENTS AS USUAL

Rhymes & times

Writing is like breathing for me
I rhyme in between heartbeats

Passage of Time

Minute by minute
The day peels itself
Shedding layer after layer
Moments of varied colour
Seamlessly revealing
Its pristine core
Ready to sprout
Into a new day
A new fragrance
That fills my olfactory senses
In ascending notes
Minute by minute…

You, me & tea

This evening, as we sat down to have tea,
It occurred to me,
How the making and having of tea,
Is a ritual as sacred as any.
It binds us together
Creating
a great camaraderie.
The many moments that we have poured
over tea,
These have been the moments that we relished
in glee.
Our life has brewed well
over several fragrant cups of tea.
Twenty years of togetherness — just you, me
and tea!
Memories of many aromatic moments
Often wafting into our present being,
add
to the notes of the day's hot cup of tea.
Some moments quickly boiled over to leave an
imprint in a jiffy,

Some were sipped in quiet contemplation,
while cherishing an accompanying cookie.
Despite the monotony of the whole ritual —
watching the tea leaves open in bubbling hot
water and patiently waiting
for the time to simmer —
One never desires to skip tea.
Calls can wait, as also other meetings,
Tea time's sacrosanct; it's a thing;
A strong bond we continue savouring,
Sipping into our joys, dissolving our differences
or simply being,
Be it Monday or Sunday,
One is never shy of the 'chai'.
Tea time
is prime time!

Mates, meets & treats

Of cat-tales
and ice cream pails,
of goat cheese pizzas
And talks of sunshine days.
Of laughter by the sea,
Friends meet with glee
and trod the memory lanes,
Giving wings to their souls' sails.
Of wind-swept hair,
merriment filling the air,
a bunch of jubilant kids jump around,
while the pals scrutinize the twinning girls'
attire,
Of spirits brimming high
and an overflowing cola float,
a diamond ring story surfaces,
And the friends raise a chai toast!

Of winks and walks
And jostling through the crowds,
Of impatience to finally relish and eat,
Some Rustom's ice cream treats!
Of deep blue skies
Canopying the greens,
The old ladies bustle past
selfie-happy, strolling teens.
Of deep discount shopping
And birthday months,
They buy some lipsticks, T-s
And some ill-fitting heels.
Of hugs-n-kisses
And future-meet promises,
A Sunday well-spent,
The ladies depart.
Young at heart,
Brisk in their gait,
They're full of beans any time of the day,
Never mind the greys!

Faltering gait

The rain paid a visit.
Its memory was locked in the still-heavy air
and the sparkling greenery everywhere.
I decided to mark my presence with a walk.
Soaking in nature's abundance,
I hoped to get back my balance,
my flair.
With a careful gait,
faltering to evade
the dried leaves and twigs
scattered here and there,
I let myself revel in the windy wilderness to my
heart's desire.
The sound of crickets filled the air,
alongside the symphony of birds,
interspersed
with random beeps, honks and blares,

the noise of the traffic plying near here.
Every person walking beside me
had their minds drenched in their cloud of
thoughts to clear.
Not a glance to throw.
Not a thought to spare.
We were like a bunch of islands floating about
our own closeted lives,
our despair.
As I navigated the puddles,
the sun — with nothing more to declare —
decided to hand over the screen to the stars.
It set unnoticed behind the clouds,
quietly retreating from those unaware.
Soon the lights in the buildings' little boxed
houses,
blinkered on in their rhythm and glare.
The events of the evening made the
waters of my mind restless,
and I took a detour.
I tried to keep pace with life,
on the ground and in the sky.
But it just passed me by.

Music of life

In gratitude
I breathe in,
In surrender,
I let go
the present and the past.
The flute is nimble,
The beat is fast.
Words form verses,
a web to the future
they cast.
The symphony plays
to the eternal rhythm.
I sway
till the music lasts.

Together we sail

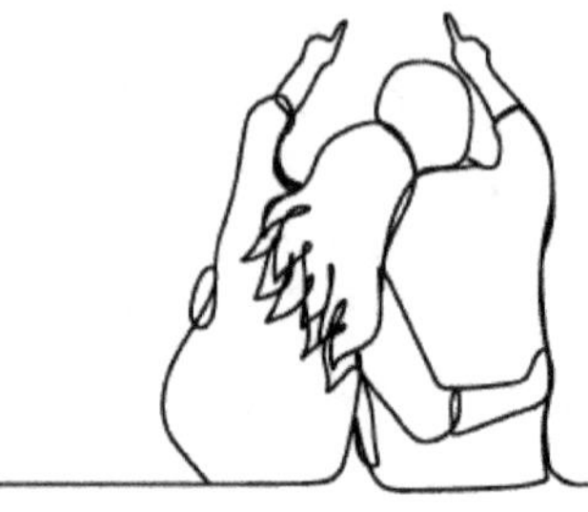

You came like spring in my life
And as we passed the days together,
The changing seasons
Didn't matter.
We've braved the winters
In the quiet warmth of our love
And when some summer days
Turned their scorching gaze
Upon our wilting lives,
The canopy of our eyelids was enough to
provide succour and shade.
At times, when the torrential tides
Threatened our lives
Our childlike dreams helped us sail through.
And when life quizzed us
With some real toughies
bizarre
Faith came in handy
Truth served as the guiding star.

Love

I moved my eyes across the skies
To paint a rainbow for you.
I then blinked to make the stars twinkle
in delight,
A welcoming view.
I beckoned a stern look
So the clouds would stay away.
With a long gaze beyond the horizon
I begged eternity to bless you.
That's what you mean to me,
That's how much I love you!

CHAPTER 4 :

NATURE AS MUSE

Wisdom

When the path appears bleak
And I strive
To find my feet,
A weed blowing in the wind
Shows me the direction.

Robin in solitude

The warmth of love pervades my heart and my
entire being,
When the air fills with the song of the Indian
robin.
Perched on a rope between two trees —
as if, undecided on its dwelling —
the robin sang loudly,
each day of spring.
The sweetness of its rendition
could potentially distract angels,
and it has broken the silence of many a siesta,
With its warbling rhythmic lilts
Like in a music fiesta.
One day, mesmerised,
I had a strong urge to ask the universe,
"For what is this bird searching?"
I quickly pulled out some tarot cards
only to find that the depressed bird

was caught in its circuitous crooning.
It was alone, looking for a mate and a new
living.
No one could perceive the sorrow behind the
bird's soulful singing.
As I looked at the bright moon that evening,
to which the bird would face and sing,
its long tail upright,
I prayed hard that the robin found a mate,
someone along with it to sing
and fly.

Each day, I would look with hope-filled eyes,
"Did the robin find a partner who could pay
heed to its cries?"
A few weeks passed
But there appeared no sign of another robin.
Its song now reeked of heartbreaking
melancholia,
But nature's networks are strong and blessed
There must be another robin in the vicinity
with whom our bird could sing in synchronicity.
Just a few days into the rain,
as the surrounding greenery
brightened the days,
healing the body's tiredness
and the soul's pains,
the skies looked plump with clouds,

The air was effervescent, with the cool breeze
swaying the trees around.
Just then I saw on the neem tree, two — not one
— robins,
singing a duet!
Each showed up, one after the other,
plonking on the branch right in front of my
windowsill;
hopping happy, swirling and chasing,
A tango of a bird couple, if you will!
Elated,
I thanked the universe,
I thanked the stars.
Nature's benevolence goes
far beyond ours…
She gives when we ask!
She gives when we ask!

Nature's symphony

When the winds began
to sing a song,
Dried leaves danced,
The trees
picked up the beats
and swayed along.
The squirrel took a break
to add to the chorus.
My heartbeats synced
with nature's symphony,
Liberating my soul
From the burden of aeons.

The sound of nature's silence

Clothed in silence,
Your light walks in to wake up the world from
its slumber.
Silent is the onset of the evening
sombre.
Quiet is the passing by of the years__
Ageing.
Where's the sound in the sprouting of a
seedling?
Neither is there a cry of joy
in a flower's blooming,
nor a whimper of sorrow in its wilting.
Silent is your act of kindness__
benevolence.
Silent is also your taking away what truly
belongs to you__
unquestionably righteous.
Silent is your communication__
granting of prayers,
reciprocal to invocations sublime.
Silent is also your tool that moves the worlds__
Time.

Yet, there's music in nature,
if one cares to hear.

The Fantail

The air was moist with the rain,
the greens turned a shade brighter
contrasting dichotomously
with the browns
set to the sound of pitter-patter.
Just then on my window pane
she fanned her tail
and twice swung around,
creating a circle of love unbound.
Thus greeting the onset of rain,
the greyish Fantail
swooned me,
leaving me enthralled
by the demonstration
of an act enchanting.
As she flew away,
my mind flew with her
only to be pulled back in
by a chorus started by
a squirrel
with the crows joining in.

Nature's treasures

In bright sunshine
leaves of the Peepal tree
shimmered like gold,
Enriching my parched soul.
A thought of being one with nature
pranced by.
I drenched my eyes
and soaked my glance
into the glistening dance
of the bejewelled beauties.

Moon mate

From behind a coconut tree
And in between rows of buildings,
As I travel on the highway
You travel with me.
At times, hidden behind a cloud,
You emerge suddenly out of the blue,
As if playing peekaboo.
Then you showed up again,
promptly perching yourself
on a dried twig of a tree,
Smiling, as I smile back at you.
Thank you
For accompanying me
Through the journey
From the time you rose,
Till the time I reached home,
And you reached

Your peak glow
On a bright
full moon night.

Sunshine

The setting rays of the sun
Threw themselves around the trees,
Embracing every nook and corner of the garden
green
With their multitude of extremities,
And bestowing light on the falling leaves,
Helping them shine with gaiety
-For the last time-
Creating a soothing sight,
Just before disappearing
To light
the moon at night.

Allure

I could see romance in the sky.
The birds flirted with the wind
And the latter gently caressed them__
unconditionally, helping them fly.
Two clouds exchanged glances amorously;
Another cloud nudged a rather nonchalant
neighbour ahead.
Looking at the courtships,
The sun blushed and set
and the sky turned crimson red.

What I learnt from a blade of grass

As I sat down on the garden bench,
to empty my cacophonous mind
and soak in the healing
amid the greens,
I glanced upon
a blade of grass just near my feet.
It stood upright;
Unafraid, unperturbed
Of being trampled
Or stomped under unknown feet.
It got its strength from the earth
its roots anchored in.
The inspiration
was from the sky,
starlit.
Taking in the light and nourishing the soil,
the grass-blade unwittingly became a conduit
between the unknown and the known.
Yet,
One among the many,
It stood its ground,
Doing its bit,
Comforting even those
who might just trample it…

Inner strength

As the dark night
imperiously
reflected its might
onto the ocean,
The waves held on
dearly
to the beautiful memories
of sunshine.
Waiting for the cycle to turn;
for the sun to rise again,
the waves in motion,
sensed their inner strength,
and became the mighty ocean.

The journey

As I walk on life's paths,
my feet randomly
gather some mud.
I walk on,
miles on miles,
crossing plains,
crossing peaks,
braving the storms,
embracing the breeze.
As I walk along green pastures,
I willy-nilly pick up some seeds.
I cross mountains, lakes and creeks.
I unknowingly
plant some flowers,
some trees.

Courage to love

An amorous interaction
between the sky and the ocean
reached a conjunction,
their borders blurred,
And the two swayed in reciprocation.
Neither understands barriers or boundaries.
Stability is a crutch used by those who limit their
dreams and their visions.
The sky and the ocean,
subtly
reflect and respect
each other's magnificence.
They happily meld into each other like a trusted
twosome.
Sacrifice is a word dreaded by the fearful.
The sky succumbs to the ocean's
vastness,
conscientiously.
It surrenders benevolently.
The drops in the ocean relinquish their haven,
their very existence,

and evaporate into oblivion.
They die,
to become the sky.

A fairy tale wish

O delightful, warm, golden
soldiers of the sun,
Take me with you
on your way back to the sky at dusk.
We'll take along with us,
the cool drops of the ocean,
the sweet sap of the blooming
daisies,
and the nectar
that dots the foreheads of the toiling farmers
tilling their land with their

ploughs.
I will come back with you at the crack of dawn,
with the blissful rain,
to bring a smile to the faces of the wrinkled
brows.

A drop of a reflected world

As round as the moon,
a circle, a symbol, a rune,
perceive it as you may,
a drop of rain
withstands gravity
as it adheres to the branch of the neem tree.
A part of the whole,
yet absolute;
a single note
in the universal rhythm,
in tune.
A whole world on its curvature,
the raindrop reflects
the sky, the stars, the clouds and the moon.
Dimensions are relative,
Gigantic or small,
inner strength is intrinsic to all.
A butterfly today
was once a cocoon.
What's sown in the ground
will emerge soon.
A drop of memory in my subconscious waters
reflects from my eyes
the light of the stars in the skies.
Nature's mysteries unravel
in unbounded, infinitesimal ways.

What connects us
are the waters of our being
that ever flow,
never die.
What I see in your eyes,
I see in the skies!

CHAPTER 5 :

Longings, nostalgia

A sign

I was despondent
Searching for you
Looking for a clue...
And then it rained

Radiant reflection

When you mark your gracious presence
in the dull confines
of my contemplative mind,
The mundane lane I tread__
Corn-stricken, thorn laden__
Turns into a fragrant garden.

A winged memory

In the morning, as I peeped out of the window,
a large brown butterfly
held my gaze for a while.
As it fluttered about,
its wings sparkled in the sunlight —
a bright brown shimmering sight.
I wondered, is it a sign?
as it swung around and disappeared,
blending into the earthy woods
leaving behind
in my mind
a magical sway
as I went about my day,
flitting from one duty to another.
It was no ordinary day
It was your remembrance day

which I honour with a chocolate cake, embossed
with pink roses,
appealing to your taste.
By midday,
the image of the butterfly was still fluttering in
my mind's bay,
I moved on to finish some other chores for the
day.
My mind was occupied as I reminisced about
my growing-up days,
I recalled some conversations
animated by you,
that would make us laugh all day!
I counted the years since you departed.
Just like that, time has flown away,
A phrase you would often stress upon and say.
In the evening, I stared into the fading
silhouettes,
hoping to catch another glimpse of the brown
butterfly,
while the sun cast its last rays.
Failing to find one,
I turned within.
I looked at your framed photo hung on the wall,
and recalled the nice holiday
where the memory was photographed.
Image of the beautiful sunset and its rays
filtering through the French windows of the
beach resort that day,

flooded my mind.
Suddenly, I wanted to see more of you.
I hurriedly looked up old pictures that were
digitally stored away.
I also played some songs you soulfully sang.
When a Hindi movie song that celebrates the
memory of love, which is
ever fragrant like a bud, like a morning breeze,
in the gardens of faith,
played,
I chanced upon your pictures from the special
holiday.
As I zoomed into the one which adorns my walls
today,
Memories gushed in like moonlight at night.
My heart was beating at presto,
outwitting the tempo of the background music.
You were sitting on an olive green sofa,
Beaming your royal smile,
with a twinkle in your eye,
And there, on the wall behind you,
was a portrait of a big brown butterfly…

Reflections

As I reflect
On the waters of my mind,
My thoughts,
Like birds
Of different kinds,
Fly by
Creating ripples,
Successively
Throwing up memories.
At intersections,
The light
Shimmers
On the surface,
Every spot
Illuminating new insights.
As I let go
Of darkness deep,
Raising my gaze
For a glimpse of eternity,
I get a felicitous peep.

A memory not meant to be

It was a narrow lane
On a hilly road
And I was pacing ahead
To visit a place
Where the air
is charged with
your memories__
Where you once walked,
Breathed
And played.
But I encountered an unexplained fog,
deep and dense,
stopping me in my tracks.
I froze, completely blinded to the path ahead,

Waiting for the fog to lift.
Passersby continued their journey
But I couldn't move an inch.
The place was just a stone's throw away.
I couldn't budge.
I stared at the fog as it engulfed me,
Overpowering me.
I decided to retreat,
Returning empty
Without the memories
I was planning to collect.
For years, this has bothered me
I could have taken a few brave steps
to pay my respects,
And to enrich my store of memories.
As life fast-tracked,
Today I leave the guilt behind.
Sagaciously though, I find,
there was a denser fog
in my mind.

Ponderance

I took a leaf from daylight
To light up some dull moments.
The trees stood as spectators
And the wind blew away the blues.
Diving deep into the depths of my mind,
I borrowed a shiny page buried under the dust of
the past,
To add some sparkle to the day's pale hues.
The present stood gazing,
While I sent out positive vibes to an uncertain
future,
To make it ring true.

Presage

The wind whispered
something in my ear
quietly, succinctly,
like a dream.
I lay unperturbed
by the message it delivered,
A premonition?
Call it what you may,
it was no ordinary day,
when you fight and make up
and laugh about it later,
blowing all your worries away.
It was clairvoyance,
the sky had merged with the earth
creating a tunnel, a flyover, if you will,
all efforts proved uphill,
tears mingled with rain showers,
emotions were on a roller coaster ride,
The time had come

for someone special to cross over to the other
side.

Past self

As I walked with measured steps
into the old building,
I walked into the past.
With strong strokes,
The wind blew my hair behind,
whispering something in my ears,
Just like it did twenty years ago.
I could see my shadow walking ahead of me,
While my mind regressed to another era.
The sun drowned in the sea so quickly,
As if, warning me against lifting the veil of the
past
"What's gone is gone."
The strong, silent walls of the building
wore a testimony of the golden days.
In their blurred reflection,
my mind saw a younger self,

Bearing a bounce in her step,
And a nascent exuberance that got consumed by
the passing years.
Nostalgia got the better of me,
The feeling was unreal,
As I relived the past,
Mixed feelings arose in my heart,
Did I really go down that stream?
It felt just like a dream.

Nostalgia

An old song,
a familiar line,
like a pleasant waft from an era gone by,
a stray thought has travelled the many
yesterdays
to appear as fresh as dew today,
wrapped in nostalgia
that nurtured it against
time's depleting effects on the mind's recall,
bringing a smile to a weary day.

Yearning

Everyday
I miss you like the Earth would
If the Sun didn't show up…

Journey from what I knew to what I know

Caged between the pages
of an old book,
My fastidious fingers
caught the grime of several years.
As I leafed through my all-time favourite,
Memories were unlatched and began to linger.
Dust particles lit up in the receding sunlight,
setting the neurons in my brain aflicker.
As I turned the pages, the clock turned back.
Faces of friends from yesteryears,
flashed in my mind.
What also began to echo,
Was the laughter
of many years ago.
The subconscious mind
geared to match
every thought with an image.
No breather!

Now, events surrounding the time I bought the
book,
came together,
each raising their heels
to show up and register.
"You have already read this book," a
self-conscious thought suddenly
pushed its way through the clutter.
"How will it help you now?" it remarked with
pomp and grandeur.
When I reached the chapter
I was looking for,
Mist of many years
got cleared.
A fresh perspective emerged from under the
cover,
My grey cells helped it unfurl.
Finally,
The oyster had created its precious pearl!

Musk musings

It was a familiar whiff
to the delight of
my olfactory senses.
The overtones of the sniff
were reminiscent
of a childhood,
memories of which
are stored as `GIF'
in my subconscious mind.
A smile began cozying up to my lips,
a rosy blush spread its charm.
Strange eyes, upper lip stiff,
glared at my mental meanderings__
propelled, perhaps, by a sylph.
For the moments
till the frolic did last,
in a crowd,
in a jiff,
my mind had wandered
to a bygone past.

Mom

With an aura
clothed in light,
You are my sun,
my moon
my whole universe.
Your love exudes
the fragrance of a thousand
blooming roses.
The nurturing embrace of your glance
feels like a pleasant walk
in ethereal gardens.

(Note: This was written on my mother's last
birthday celebration)

Book intro:

This book is a collection of poems composed by Namrata Singh, a former journalist who followed her life's calling to pursue tarot card reading. The range of topics is diverse and covers the poet's deep connection with nature, events and occurrences in her day-to-day life, and her life's philosophy and spirituality.

Being intuitive and imaginative, the poet can relate to even the most monotonous events in life and convert them into beautiful poetry.

Be it tea time or the inspiration she draws from a blade of grass, the poet effortlessly reveals her versatility while bridging the gap between the mundane and the spiritual.

With a philosophical bent of mind, the poet provides contours to the arcane, unseen aspects of life in some of her poems, while in others that deal with the day-to-day physical world, she provides a thought-provoking subtle nuance.

The poems in this book are not only engaging but stimulating as well. The reader would find it easy to grasp the meaning of the poems, which also have a rhythmic flow to them.

Many would be encouraged to dig deeper into life's esoteric aspects and connect with their higher selves

The message conveyed through this collection of poems is that there's more to life, prodding the reader to look for that extraordinary, sublime streak in the ordinary, even as we progress in our journey to fathom the otherworldly.

About the author:

Namrata Singh is an intuitive tarot card reader who was earlier a journalist. Her career journey has moved from writing news stories and features for *The Times of India* to reading cards for people. Tarot has been a life's calling for Namrata, and it is now defining the turning point in her life. What has remained constant in Namrata's life are moments spent in quiet contemplation and poetry writing. Living with her husband amidst the sylvan surroundings of Vikhroli, a suburb in Mumbai, Namrata finds inspiration to write a poem on topics that range from a blade of grass to a raindrop to the whole universe.

To learn more about the author, visit her website, www.OnTheTarotTable.com.

You can follow her on Instagram @OnTheTarotTable.